THIS BOOK BELONGS TO
ALLISON BROWN

PLEASE DO NOT REMOVE FROM CLASS

THANK YOU!

# LOOKING **BACK**

# CLOTHES AND FASHION

## JOANNE JESSOP

# LOOKING BACK

CLOTHES AND FASHION

FAMILY LIFE

FOOD

HOLIDAYS AND PASTIMES

TRANSPORT

WORK

Book editor: Joanna Housley
Series editor: Rosemary Ashley
Designer: Bruce Low

First published in 1991 by
Wayland (Publishers) Limited
61 Western Road, Hove
East Sussex, BN3 1JD, England

**British Library Cataloguing in Publication Data**
Jessop, Joanne
Clothes and fashion.
1. British costume, history
I. Title    II. Series
391.00941

ISBN 0–7502–0129–0

Typeset by DP Press Limited
Printed in Italy by G Canale C.S.p.A., Turin
Bound in Belgium by Casterman S.A.

# CONTENTS

# INTRODUCTION

When you look at photographs of people from the past you can usually tell by the clothes they are wearing when the picture was taken. At the beginning of this century, people wore far more clothing than they do today, mainly because it was one of the best ways of keeping warm.
A photograph taken then would show women in long skirts, men in dark suits and high, stiff collars. Children were usually dressed as smaller versions of their parents – the boys in suits and the girls in frilly dresses.

Styles have changed a great deal since then. Clothing and fashions have been greatly influenced by changes in the world around us. For example, during the First and Second World Wars, when materials were in short supply, styles became simpler and more practical. In times of greater prosperity, fashions became more frivolous.

Clothes have also been adapted to suit changing lifestyles. As people began to be interested in outdoor activities, clothing became more casual. Women began to take a more active part

*Edwardian men and women wore elaborate, formal dress for evenings out.*

in society, and so their clothes became less restrictive, giving them greater freedom of movement.

The invention of synthetic materials in the mid-twentieth century and improvements in clothing manufacture have increased the range of inexpensive, yet fashionable, clothing now available in the shops. Improved heating in homes and schools means we no longer have to wear so many layers of clothing to keep warm.

*By the 1920s, feminine curves were replaced with straight lines.*

Looking back on this century we can see that each period had its own particular style. At the turn of the century women wore corsets to shape their figures and their skirts reached the ground. Fashionable women of the 1920s wore short, straight skirts and adopted a boyish look. The young people of the 1960s wore mini skirts and flared trousers. You may look at pictures of people wearing these clothes and think them silly and old-fashioned, but they were the acceptable fashions at that time. Perhaps people in the future will also be amused when they look back at the clothes you are wearing today.

*The Teddy Boy look, hippy fashions, and mini-skirt from the 1950s and '60s.*

# 1  THE EDWARDIANS

The twentieth century began with a new king. In January 1901, King Edward VII came to the throne after the death of Queen Victoria. The Edwardian era saw many exciting changes. The motor car was beginning to replace the horse and carriage, and the first aeroplanes took to the skies. The London Underground was built, and the telephone and telegraph came into service. There was a general mood of hopefulness and enjoyment, which was reflected in Edwardian fashions.

Clothes were taken very seriously by the upper-class Edwardians. It was important to wear the 'right' clothes. What was suitable dress in the country was not suitable for town wear; what was suitable for daytime was not suitable for evening wear. Clothes were very elaborate, and only rich people had the money and leisure time required to dress fashionably. They carefully copied the latest styles produced by the Paris fashion houses or those worn by the royal court. The well-dressed Edwardian lady was

*This Edwardian couple are dressed in formal daytime clothes.*

*An Edwardian lady needed a maid's help when dressing.*

tightly bound up in a corset that pushed her bust forward and her hips backwards, to give her the popular S-shape curve. Skirts touched the ground, sometimes with trains trailing behind. For daytime wear, sleeves were long and collars were nearly up to the ears; but in the evening, gowns were cut low and arms were bare. Dressed in her silks and laces, embroidery and ribbons, the Edwardian lady was a symbol of the splendour of the age.

Men did not dress as elaborately as women. However, with their long undergarments, high, stiff collars, waistcoats and

*Edwardian women wore tight corsets to achieve an 'hour glass' figure.*

thick suits, Edwardian men would seem extremely overdressed to us. A frock coat or morning coat, both reaching well down the thigh, and top hat was the correct daytime wear. The three-piece lounge suit, which has become today's business suit, was worn for less formal occasions in town or for country wear.

Casual sportswear for men was plus fours or wide-legged trousers and Fair Isle sweaters. The standard oufit for driving in open motor cars was a leather, fur-lined jacket or a cape, a cloth cap with ear flaps, and goggles. Women passengers wore dust-proof veils to protect their elegant hairstyles and hats.

*Children's clothes of the early 1900s seem formal and awkward to us.*

'... all girls' clothing of the period appeared to be designed by their elders on the assumption that decency consisted in leaving exposed to the sun and air no part of the body that could possibly be covered ... [We were] wrapped up in woollen combinations, black cashmere stockings, 'liberty' bodice, dark stockinette knickers, flannel petticoat and often ... a long-sleeved, high-necked woollen 'spencer' ... For cricket and tennis matches, even in the baking summer of 1911, we still wore the flowing skirts and high-necked blouses, with our heavy hair braided in pigtails ...'

Vera Brittain,
*Testament of Youth*, 1933

Cycling was one of the few sporting activities enjoyed by Edwardian women. Ankle-length skirts or divided skirts became the fashion for cycling. Some women wore breeches, but these were usually hidden under a skirt with flaps that could be buttoned out of the way when cycling. A few daring young women shocked their elders by wearing bloomers. These were full, puffed-out knickerbockers, fastened below the knee with garters, on top of black woollen stockings.

*'My long skirt was a nuisance and even a danger. It is an unpleasant experience to be hurled on to stone setts [paving blocks] and find that one's skirt has been so tightly wound round the pedal that one cannot even get up enough to unwind it.'*
Helena Swanwick referring to her cycling experiences, *I Have Been Young*, 1935

*Even on the tennis court, Edwardian clothes were elaborate and kept the body covered from head to toe.*

But not everyone in Edwardian society dressed in the latest fashions. The poor, who made up the majority of the population, could not afford to follow fashions. They had to make do with rough, dull-coloured clothes. A working-class man's clothes usually consisted of a jacket, corduroy trousers, a flat cap and thick heavy boots or wooden clogs. His wife would often make do with a ragged dress. Since she rarely left the house, there was little need to waste money on her clothes. On her trips to the local shops she would cover her shabby dress with a shawl or an old blanket.

*'[The miners' wives were] dumpy shawled women with their sacking aprons and the heavy black clogs, kneeling in the cindery mud and bitter wind searching eagerly for tiny chips of coal.'*

George Orwell
*Road to Wigan Pier*, 1937

It was a common sight to see children going barefoot or wearing ill-fitting boots – new shoes were a luxury that many families simply could not afford.

*The poor had little time or money to spend on fashionable clothes.*

*This magazine advertisement for women's dresses appeared in 1911. By this time skirts had become very narrow.*

The poor were not the only ones who remained outside fashion. Some middle-class women preferred more sensible clothes that would give them greater freedom of movement, especially if they sought work and independence. These 'New Women', as they were called, resented the time and money spent on fashion. They refused to wear corsets, which were not only uncomfortable, but also unhealthy because they were so tight. Instead of fashionable clothing, they chose plain blouses, jackets and flared skirts that just cleared the ground.

The New Women's preference for sensible clothing was soon reflected in high fashion. Paris designers began to do away with frills in favour of straight, simple styles. Fashionable women still wore corsets, but their bodies were freed from the S-shape and allowed to look more natural. However, many fashions still restricted women's ability to move easily. The straight, narrow skirt became more and more narrow, until around 1910 the 'hobble skirt' entered the fashion scene. It got its name from the fact that it restricted walking to a mere hobble.

# 2  SOCIAL CHANGE

The extravagance of the Edwardian age ended with the outbreak of the First World War in 1914. In a country at war, there was less time or money for fashionable clothes, even among the rich. As women took over the men's jobs in factories and offices they needed styles that did not restrict movement. Dresses became loose and easy-fitting; skirts became shorter. Looking back, these clothes still seem awkward to us, but they were much freer than anything women had worn before. Women who joined the Land Army of farm workers even wore trousers. This alarmed many people, who feared that women in trousers might not behave in a 'ladylike' way.

The men who stayed at home during the war made do with the clothes they already had, rather than waste materials on new ones. The extravagant frock coat and top hat were disappearing forever.

Throughout the war, women were busy knitting jumpers,

*Members of the Women's Land Army.*

'You are doing men's work and so you're dressed rather like a man, but remember just because you wear a smock and breeches you should take care to behave like a British girl who expects chivalry and respect from everyone she meets.'
Extract from the
*Women's Land Army Handbook,* 1917

UNE VILLA ET UN CŒUR

*By the mid-1920s, some daring young women were wearing knee-length skirts.*

and put aside the memories of war and hardship. They became known as the 'Gay Young Things' and shocked their elders with their daring new styles. Young women cut their hair and shortened their skirts. The waistline dropped to the hips, and the bustline was flattened to give a straight, boyish look. Make-up became acceptable for the first time. By the mid-1920s, skirts were up to the knee – never before had women exposed so much of their legs.

Men's clothing grew less formal. The lounge suit became normal daytime wear and shirts with soft collars replaced the stiff, detachable collar. Trouser legs became wider – the 'Oxford bags' of the mid-1920s were up to 60 cm wide at the hem. Jackets were double-breasted and had padded shoulders. Knitted V-necked pullovers began to replace waistcoats. Children's clothes, too, became less formal. Girls' fashions followed those of their mothers, with loose, low-waisted dresses, skirts and knitted jumpers. Boys wore short trousers until about the age of eleven, when they were allowed to wear their 'longs'.

In 1929 the crash of the New York stock exchange brought about a worldwide economic

socks and scarves for the troops. Until that time, few people wore knitted jumpers. However, after the war, jumpers came into fashion for everyone and have remained popular ever since.

When the war ended in 1918, thousands of soldiers came home to be faced with unemployment. There was peace but not prosperity. Most people had little money to spend on clothes. However, for those young people lucky enough to afford it, the post-war period was a time to have fun

*Casual dress for men in the 1920s was plus fours and 'Oxford bags'.*

depression. For the thousands of unemployed men and their families, there was no question of following fashion. Even for the rich, fashions became less frivolous. Dresses had a softer, more feminine look; they were worn longer and nipped in at the waist. One of the greatest influences on the fashions of the 1930s was the cinema. The clothes worn by film stars were seen and copied by millions.

*Film stars such as Greta Garbo set fashions in the 1930s.*

For walks in the countryside, a popular pastime in the 1930s, men dressed comfortably in open-necked shirts and shorts. Women started to wear trousers in the countryside, but never in town. Female bodies became more exposed than ever before. Backless bathing costumes could be seen at the seaside, and suntans became fashionable for the first time. For evening wear, backless gowns made from smooth, clinging fabrics were popular throughout the 1930s.

*A clothing coupon book. Clothes were rationed during the Second World War because of shortages of materials.*

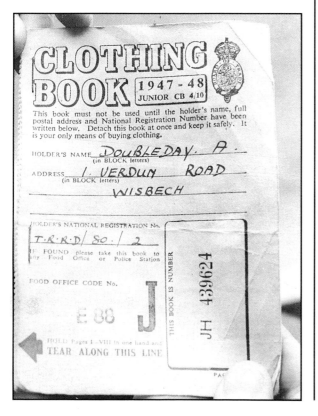

By 1939, Britain was once more at war. The Second World War, like the First, was to have far-reaching consequences on all aspects of life, including fashions. Clothes, like many other items, were in short supply and had to be rationed. Each person had forty clothing coupons a year. Coupons had to be handed over with each purchase. A suit alone used up eighteen coupons. Government restrictions, known as the Utility Scheme, limited the amount of fabric manufacturers could use in making a garment. Utility Scheme clothing was hard-wearing, with simple styles and no frills. Women's skirts were short and straight. Men's trousers were narrow, with no turn-ups or pleats; jackets were single-breasted with no buttons on the cuffs and no pocket flaps.

Once more, as the men went to war, women started taking over their jobs in offices and factories. Trousers and pullovers became popular wear for women because they were practical and warm. Overalls had an added advantage; they could be purchased without clothing coupons.

Headscarves were worn by women factory workers to keep their hair from being caught in

'People found inventive ways of getting around wartime rationing. Women made dresses out of curtains and furnishing material, which was not rationed. Blankets were made into coats, blackout material into skirts, and parachute silks were secretly used to make underwear. Old sweaters were unravelled and the yarn re-used, and old clothes re-made into new ones. It was considered everyone's patriotic duty to make clothes last as long as possible.'

A woman recalling
life during the
Second World War

*Some women painted their legs when stockings were hard to get.*

*With so many men away at war, women were encouraged to work in the factories.*

> *'I had a navy blue coat, nipped in at the waist and ankle length with a very full skirt. With it I wore strap-round-the-ankle lizard-skin, wedge-heeled shoes and huge fur-backed gloves. Of course, I always wore a hat, that goes without saying.'*
> A woman talking about the New Look, quoted in *Out of the Doll's House* by Angela Holdsworth, 1988

the machinery. They had previously been worn only in the country, but were soon seen everywhere, and have been worn ever since. The 'glamour band' was a scarf worn twisted round the head and tied in a roll at the front, completely covering the hair except for a front curl. The 'snood' was a loose, bag-like net that held the hair.

Some fashions from the armed forces, such as the seaman's woollen roll-neck sweater and hooded duffle coat and the airman's leather jacket, were adapted for leisure wear after the war.

*The 'New Look' fashions of the post-war period featured full skirts, soft lines and nipped-in waists.*

When the war ended, 'New Look' fashion was launched in Paris. It featured soft curves and long, full skirts – a welcome change to the skimpy wartime clothes. These styles made women look more feminine than the severe clothes they had worn during the war. However, there were strong protests against the New Look styles by those who felt it was wrong to use so much material on full skirts when many people still did not have enough to eat.

# 3 CLOTHES AND TECHNOLOGY

Another major influence on clothes and fashions this century has been the technical innovations in the clothing industry.

At the beginning of this century, most clothes were handsewn by wives, mothers, grandmothers and aunts at home, or by a local dressmaker or tailor. The production of clothing on a large scale first became necessary during the First World War, when there was a sudden demand for thousands of soldiers' uniforms. Factories geared up to meet this demand. Labour-saving machines such as the mechanical cutter were used to increase production. After the war, factory production switched to ready-to-wear fashions, which were in great demand among the growing number of working women.

Home dressmaking decreased as a result of mass-production of clothing, but is still popular with some people because it allows them to choose their own colours and styles that may not be available in shops.

Hand-in-hand with changes in the manufacturing methods came the development of synthetic

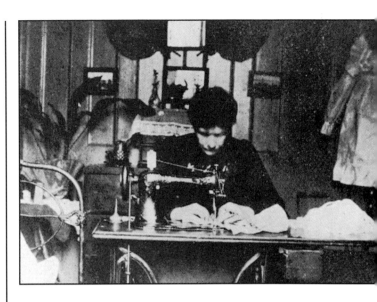

*A dressmaker working at home in 1906.*

'[Women worked in] the various 'domestic' and 'sweated' trades: dressmaking, millinery . . . and so on. These trades were carried on either in a woman's own home, or in some tiny crowded workshop, beyond the reach of the overworked factory inspectorate; usually on piecework, the women were paid [very low] sums for producing quantities of goods which required inhumanly long hours of work.'
Women at War,
1914–1918 by
Arthur Marwick, 1977

*A craftsman weaves woollen cloth on a hand loom.*

fabrics. In the past, most clothes were made from natural fibres such as cotton, linen, silk or wool. With the introduction of synthetics, manufacturers were able to produce inexpensive yet fashionable clothes in huge quantities. Fashion was no longer just for the rich.

Rayon, a fibre made from plant cellulose, came into general use in the 1920s. Rayon dresses had the glamour of silk but were much cheaper. Skin-coloured, lightweight rayon stockings soon

'In the 1950s, all my shirts were drip-dry nylon. I would wash them by hand and then hang them up to dry in the bathroom. It was great, I never had to iron them, which was a great advantage for a working bachelor. However, those shirts were never as cool as cotton and not nearly as absorbent.'
A man discussing clothes of the 1950s

replaced the dark woollen or cotton stockings that had been part of every woman's wardrobe.

Nylon, the first fully synthetic fibre, was developed in the late 1930s. Sheer 'nylons', which became available in Britain after the Second World War, were much preferred to rayon stockings. Lightweight nylon shirts, dresses and underwear were also instantly popular.

Other synthetics soon followed. Polyester was used to make

*Alluring...Enduring...*

*Wolsey*
**nylons**

Wolsey Limited Leicester

*Nylon, the first fully synthetic fibre, was used in stockings.*

clothes that did not crease, and acrylic yarns were used in thick, soft jumpers. Lycra, an elastic fibre that dries quickly, is a recent development. It is used to make swimwear and underwear.

Synthetic fibres have many advantages over natural fibres. They are generally stronger and

'... 'Viyella'. It'll keep you on good terms with your purse, for in spite of its soft texture and light-hearted colours 'Viyella' wears tirelessly and washes like a kitten's ear.'
Advertisement for 'Viyella', promoting this natural wool fabric in competition with synthetic materials.

*Lycra is used to make stretchy clothes for cycling and other sports.*

last longer. Clothes made from synthetic materials are also easier to wash and iron, and they can be dyed so that colours never run. But synthetics also have disadvantages. Acrylics are not as warm as wool; nylon clothes hold in the heat and sweat of the body. However, today's better-quality synthetics and synthetic and natural fibre mixes provide a more natural look and feel.

Clothing manufacture is continually being up-dated. Many complex tasks that were once done by hand are now done by machine. Even zips can be sewn into jeans by machine – at a rate of sixty zips an hour! Computers ensure that patterns are laid on the fabric with the least waste, and garments can even be sewn up by robot sewing machines.

*Modern cutting machines can cut up to a hundred thicknesses of fabric at once.*

# 4 FASHION AND LIFESTYLE

With the greater prosperity of the 1950s, more people could afford to dress fashionably. Styles were still rather more formal than they are today. Skirts were 'pencil thin' or very full – both rather uncomfortable styles. Most women still wore girdles to make their bodies look firmer. Men's fashions tended to go back to pre-war styles. Shoulders were broad but jackets were narrow to fit neatly around the hips. Trousers were wide with turn-ups. Hats were essential.

More casual styles such as shirtwaister dresses, sweaters and denim jeans were beginning to appear on the fashion scene.

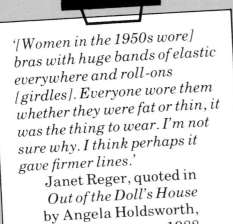

*'[Women in the 1950s wore] bras with huge bands of elastic everywhere and roll-ons [girdles]. Everyone wore them whether they were fat or thin, it was the thing to wear. I'm not sure why. I think perhaps it gave firmer lines.'*
Janet Reger, quoted in *Out of the Doll's House* by Angela Holdsworth, 1988

*In the 1950s, skirts were either extremely full or very narrow, as shown here.*

However, the most startling development of the 1950s was the idea of special fashions for the young. Teenagers of the 1950s had more money and greater freedom than ever before, and for the first time this allowed them to develop their own styles more than in the past. Most remarkable was the 'Teddy Boy' look that copied the styles of the Edwardian age. Teddy Boys were usually young, working class boys. They wore tight 'drainpipe' trousers, long jackets with padded shoulders, embroidered waistcoats, and bootlace-thin ties.

The 1960s were a time when society was generally more open to change and new ideas than in previous years. Young people

*'My girlfriend and I would get dressed up every Saturday night and go dancing. I was a real Teddy Boy. My jacket reached to my knees and had wide padded shoulders. I wore an embroidered waistcoat and drainpipe trousers. My shoes had thick crepe soles. I spent a lot of time grooming and greasing my hair. I wore it long and swept back with a quiff at the front. My girlfriend's dresses had full skirts over lots of stiffened petticoats, and she wore stiletto heels. It was like a uniform – all our friends wore similar clothes.'*

A man recalling his teenage years in the 1950s

*A 'Teddy Boy' in 1954, wearing a long Edwardian-style jacket, straight trousers and a narrow tie.*

wanted to break away from the standards and rules of the past and wear what they liked. Colourful and unusual clothes with wild designs were worn by men as well as women. The most notable styles were mini skirts, introduced by designer Mary Quant, and flared trousers. Like the film stars of the 1930s, pop stars had a great influence on fashions for the young. The Beatles style of Chelsea boots (men's boots with elastic sides) and round-necked jackets were copied all over the world.

*Popular mini-skirts were seen everywhere by 1968.*

By the late 1960s, the mood of exuberance had begun to fade and there was a general slow-down in the economy. Many young people rejected the materialistic lifestyle of the time and adopted alternative ways of living. The hippies, who 'dropped out' of mainstream society, experimented with clashing colours and styles from other

*Rock groups like 'The Who' set trends in the 1960s.*

*Hippies wore beads, headbands, flared trousers and embroidery.*

cultures. The fashions of the 1970s reflected these trends. The midi and maxi appeared as alternatives to the mini skirt. Frills and lace, and the 'country' look became popular through the designs of Laura Ashley. Both men and women wore wedge heels and platform shoes.

In the late 1970s, the punk movement began as an expression of rebellion among young people, many of whom faced unemployment. Punk fashions were deliberately ugly, aggressive and bizarre. Clothes were mostly black and tattered, and often had metal studs and safety pins on them.

A desire for healthier living and physical fitness during the late 1970s and 1980s brought with it a demand for loose, comfortable clothing. Colour coordinated jogging suits, leotards and leggings formed a popular new sporty look.

Children's clothing has changed drastically this century as a result of changes in attitudes. Fashions for children began to change in the 1930s, when it was accepted that they needed clothes in which it was easy to run about and play. As a result children's clothes became less elaborate and

*Outrageous hairstyles were part of the bizarre and aggressive punk fashions in the late 1970s.*

more practical. T-shirts were introduced in the late 1940s and were an immediate hit. But even as late as the 1950s, boys under 12 wore short trousers, and girls wore either dresses or skirts and blouses, even for play.

Today, children's clothing is fashionable yet hard-wearing and easy to care for. Children are able to choose from a wide variety of colourful and interesting styles. Nevertheless, the fashion favourite with most young people is jeans and a T-shirt or sweater.

*Today, children's clothes are colourful and attractive, as well as comfortable and practical.*

27

# 5  CLOTHES TODAY

Looking back over the twentieth century, we can see many changes in clothes and fashions. We have gone from the formal styles and the strict dress rules of Edwardian times to the openness and relaxed attitude towards clothes of the 1990s. Clothes today are more casual and fashions are freer than ever before. There is no one 'look' that is considered to be the latest fashion. People now choose their clothes to suit their personalities and lifestyles rather than follow fashion trends. As a result, a far greater variety of styles is seen than at any other time this century.

Fur coats were worn by many people in Britain at the start of the century, but now the idea of killing animals just for the sake of fashion has become very unpopular. As early as 1913 the Women's Institute stated that they did not like the idea of wearing animal furs. But it was not until the 1980s that public disapproval became so insistent that fur shops closed through lack of demand for their clothing.

*Physical fitness activities have created a demand for sporty, comfortable clothes.*

As women move into higher positions in business, the idea of 'dressing for success' or 'power dressing' has developed. This means wearing smart, tidy outfits that make a businesswoman look more professional than she would look in casual clothes.

Fashions are becoming more international than ever before. People take fashion ideas from other cultures as they travel to different countries – for instance, Indian cotton skirts and blouses, Moroccan fabrics, and Indonesian batiks have become part of the fashion scene. Paris is no longer the centre for new ideas; many of today's fashions are inspired by designers from London, New York and Tokyo.

Clothes will continue to change and fashions will come and go, in response to changes in the world around us. No doubt what you are wearing today will seem outdated a few years from now.

*Jeans remain a fashion favourite with most young people today.*

# GLOSSARY

**Absorbent**  Able to soak up liquid.

**Batik**  A process of printing fabric in which parts not to be dyed are covered by wax.

**Breeches**  Trousers that reach just below the knee.

**Cellulose**  The main part of the cell walls of all plants.

**Combinations**  A one-piece woollen undergarment with long sleeves and legs.

**Corset**  A tight-fitting, rigid woman's undergarment that moulds the figure and squeezes in the waist.

**Denim**  A cotton fabric used originally for work clothes but later adopted for men's, women's and children's jeans.

**Economic depression**  A period when business activity slows down and there is high unemployment, rising prices and low wages.

**Fair Islc sweater**  A sweater knitted in a multi-coloured pattern.

**Fashion house**  A place where fashionable clothes are designed, made and sold.

**Frock coat**  A double-breasted coat with full skirt that reaches to the knees in the front and back.

**Girdle**  Elastic underwear worn to support or mould the waist and hips.

**Hippy**  A person (especially in the 1960s) whose behaviour and appearance implies a rebellion against conventional society.

**Kaftan**  A loose, full-length, long-sleeved tunic, originally worn in Arab countries.

**Knickerbockers**  Baggy, below-the-knee trousers.

**Liberty bodice**  A thick cotton vest formerly worn by children.

**Mass produce**  To manufacture large numbers of identical products using a series of mechanical processes.

**Maxi**  An ankle-length skirt briefly fashionable in the 1970s.

**Midi**  A mid-calf-length skirt fashionable in the 1970s.

**Morning coat**  A coat with the front cut away and long tails at the back.

**Petticoat**  An underskirt often trimmed at the hemline with lace and ruffles.

**Piecework**  Work that is paid for according to how much is made.

**Plus fours**  Knickerbockers reaching to four inches below the knees.

**Prosperity**  Success or wealth.

**Quiff**  A lock of hair either pressed down over the forehead or brushed up from the brow.

**Ready-to-wear**  Clothing produced in a factory for a mass market rather than made by hand to suit the individual.

**Shingle haircut**  A short-cropped hairstyle popular with women in the 1920s.

**Spencer**  A short jacket of an early nineteenth-century style.

**Stiletto heels**  Very high, thin heels that taper to a point; named after the dagger they resemble.

**Synthetic**  Not natural. Synthetic fibres are made by forcing a chemical mixture through tiny holes to make long thin threads.

**Viyella**  A soft fabric made of wool and cotton.

**Waistcoat**  A close-fitting jacket without sleeves.

# IMPORTANT DATES

**1914–1918** First World War: more practical clothing for women doing men's jobs

**1929** Crash of New York stock exchange

**1938** Invention of nylon in USA

**1939–45** Second World War: women again doing men's work, women wearing trousers became very common

**1941** Clothes rationed and Utility Scheme introduced

**1947** Parisian designer Christian Dior launches the 'New Look'

**1949** Clothing rationing ends

**1953** Utility Scheme ends

**1965** Mini-skirt launched by designer Mary Quant

# BOOKS TO READ

*Exploring Clothes* by Brenda Ralph Lewis (Wayland, 1988)

*Costume in Context Series* by Jennifer Ruby (B.T. Batsford, 1988) (This series contains many books on the clothes of different periods in history.)

*Costumes and Clothes* by Jean Cooke (Wayland, 1986)

*Just Look at Clothes* by Brenda Ralph Lewis (Macdonald Educational, 1986)

*History of Costume* by Tim Healey (Macdonald Educational, 1977)

*Twentieth Century Fashion* by Eleanor Van Zandt (Wayland, 1988)

*Costume and Fashion, a Concise History* by James Laver (Thames and Hudson, 1982)

## ACKNOWLEDGEMENTS

The following quotations are reprinted by permission of BBC Enterprises Ltd from *Out of the Doll's House* by Angela Holdsworth; Century Hutchinson from *We Danced all Night* by Barbara Cartland; Croom Helm Publishers from *Women at War, 1914–1918* by Arthur Marwick; Victor Gollancz Ltd from *I Have Been Young* by Helena Swanwick; Virago Press from *Testament of Youth* by Vera Brittain.

# INDEX

## PICTURE ACKNOWLEDGEMENTS

The publishers wish to thank the following for providing the photographs in this book: Bridgeman Art Libary cover, 5 (top); E T Archives 17; Mary Evans Picture Library 4, 7 (bottom), 8, 13, 19, 21; Eye Ubiquitous 29; Hulton-Deutsch Collection 5 (bottom), 6, 7 (top), 9, 10, 11, 14 (both), 16, 23, 24; Popperfoto 26, 27 (top); Sefton Photo Library 22 (bottom); Topham Picture Library 12, 15, 18, 25 (both), 28; Wayland Picture Library 20, 22 (top), 27 (bottom, Woodcock).